Stepping Through History

THE POST

PEGGY BURNS

Wayland

Stepping Through History

Money
The News
The Post
Shops and Markets
Travel
Writing

Series editor: Vanessa Cummins

Book editors: Marcella Forster and Vanessa Cummins

Series designer: John Christopher

© Copyright 1994 Wayland (Publishers) Limited

First published in 1994 by Wayland (Publishers) Limited
61 Western Road, Hove, East Sussex BN3 1JD, England.

British Library Cataloguing in Publication Data
Burns, Peggy
Post. – (Stepping Through History Series)
I. Title II. Series
383.009

ISBN 0-7502-1136-9

Picture Acknowledgements

The Publishers would like to thank the following for allowing their pictures to be used in this book: Bridgeman 4; British Museum 6; J. Allan Cash 19 (below), 26 (inset); Chapel Studios 5; Bruce Coleman (Hans Reinhard) 23 (inset); C W Editorial 27; Durham School of Oriental Studies 7; Mary Evans 7, 9, 11, 13 (above), 14 (both), 15 (above), 22 (below), 23 (top and bottom), 25; Eye Ubiquitous 22 (above), 28 (above), 29; Stanley Gibbons 28 (below); Ron Hall 18 (above), 19 (above); Peter Newark 8, 10 (above), 12, 13 (below), 20, 21; Portsmouth Stamp Shop 17 (both); The British Post Office title page, 10 (below), 16, 18 (below), 24, 25, 26 (main pic), 30 (middle); John Ruffle 7 (above); Wayland contents page 15 (below), 30 (top and bottom). Maps on pages 6, 20 and 25 by John Yates.

Typeset by Strong Silent Type
Printed and bound in Italy by G. Canale & C.S.p.A., Turin

CONTENTS

GOODBYE FOREVER

Getting letters from friends and family is exciting – especially on a birthday. We all look forward to the post arriving.

But how did people send letters to each other before there were postal workers and post offices?

Usually they didn't. Long ago few people could read or write. There were no Christmas or birthday cards, and there were no telephones. Only the rich could afford to pay a messenger to deliver a letter.

In the seventeenth century many people left Europe to settle in America, 4,800 kilometres across the Atlantic Ocean.

Because there was no post between Europe and America, most of them said goodbye forever to the friends and family they left behind.

In the nineteenth century many Europeans emigrated to the USA and Australia. A six-month journey by sea separated the early Australian settlers from the friends they left behind.

Post boxes near Millicent, South Australia.

HOW THE POST BEGAN

Kings and emperors have always had messengers to carry letters for them. In the past letters were written on tablets of wax, clay and bronze or on papyrus. Sometimes messages were simply memorized.

Around 500 BC Cyrus, the Emperor of Persia, created the longest postal route in ancient times to carry royal commands across his kingdom. These were written in wet clay which dried into tablets. These were then carried in 'clay envelopes'.

Clay 'letters' and 'envelopes' were written in the wedge-shaped script of ancient Persia.

Stations, or 'posts', were set up between the cities of Sardis and Susa. Now these cities are found in modern Turkey and Iran. The posts were built one day's journey apart, and each had fresh riders and horses. The route was 542 kilometres long and even crossed deserts, linking one oasis with the next.

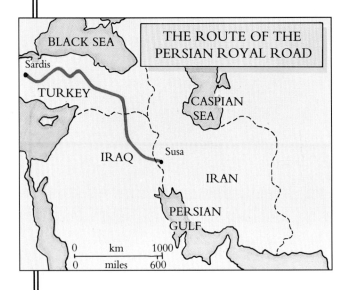

THE ROUTE OF THE PERSIAN ROYAL ROAD

BLACK SEA
Sardis
TURKEY
CASPIAN SEA
IRAQ
Susa
IRAN
PERSIAN GULF
0 km 1000
0 miles 600

Left: The route between Sardis and Susa was used so much on the Emperor's business that it became known as the 'Royal Road'.

Ruins of Persepolis, imperial city of ancient Persia.

A tired messenger, who might have been riding hard all night, would arrive at a post with letters and pass them on to another rider, who would hurry with them to the next 'post'. This carried on until the letters reached their journey's end. Over many years this process came to be known as the 'post', particularly in Britain.

This idea of posting riders and horses at regular intervals to carry letters swiftly was copied by many countries.

A French express rider in the mid nineteenth century races across country with urgent mail.

ROYAL MAIL

In AD 98 the Romans ruled much of what is now Europe. They set up an imperial postal system, but only the Emperor could use it. Private companies carried ordinary people's letters.

A picture showing Marco Polo, the Italian explorer, bringing gifts to the Chinese Emperor, Khublai Khan.

After the fall of Rome in AD 475 the Romans' postal system in Europe came to an end. However very gradually routes were set up again. During the eleventh century many monasteries and universities were opened, and each developed its own messenger service. Merchants also set up private postal routes.

Countries, such as Russia and Japan, had postal systems too. When Marco Polo, the Italian explorer, visited China in the thirteenth century, he found an excellent postal service with 25,000 posting stations across the country – but again, for the emperor's use only.

During the fifteenth and sixteenth centuries, most European rulers set up their own royal mail. Postal links were made between the countries of Germany, Austria, Belgium, France, Spain and Italy.

In Britain innkeepers often provided guides to help post riders find

The royal mail took six days to be delivered from Falmouth to London under armed guard in 1833.

addresses. The roads were dreadful, there were very few signposts and, before the nineteenth century, there were no street addresses. For instance a letter might be addressed to 'Edward Fuller, opposite the Goldsmith's'.

Although Britain had had a royal postal system for hundreds of years, it was not really organized until 1635, when a postal route was set up between London and Edinburgh. This was open to the public. The trip to Scotland took three days.

Mail coaches faced danger from the weather as well as from highwaymen.

As the amount of mail increased and began to include valuables and heavy parcels, mail coaches gradually took over from riders and foot messengers. Better roads were built, and by the end of the eighteenth century, sixteen mail coaches were leaving the General Post Office in London every day, each with an armed guard. When the mail coach arrived in a town, the postal worker would blow a bugle or ring a bell to tell people to come and get their letters.

A post boy in 1800.

In Britain every letter, once it was posted, became the property of the king or queen until it was delivered to the person to whom it was addressed. Nobody else was allowed to open any letters except an officer of the government who was investigating a crime.

THE CAPTURE OF DICK TURPIN

When a man who gave his name as John Palmer was arrested in Yorkshire in 1739 for stealing horses, no one knew his real name was Dick Turpin. He was a well-known British highwayman who was wanted by the police for robbing travellers on the road.

While in prison, he wrote to his brother in Essex. The postmaster there recognized the hand-writing. He had been Turpin's school teacher! He opened the letter, read it, and hurried north with the news that they had caught the highwayman.

The post-master was given a reward, and Dick Turpin was hanged.

A painting of Dick Turpin.

MAIL ON THE MOVE

The invention of the steam engine played an important role in moving mail more swiftly, both on land and by sea.

The average speed of overland mail in the seventeenth and eighteenth centuries was 6.4 kilometres an hour, the rate at which a horse could pull a coach. All that changed with the building of the first railways. By 1838 mail was being carried by steam train in Britain, and long-distance trains were fitted with postal sorting offices to make the post even faster.

A US express train, painted in 1859.

Non-stop mail trains picked up and dropped off mail bags.

Specialized mail-coaches were first introduced between Chicago and Iowa in 1864. Trains from New York to Chicago were robbed so often that steel-armoured mail coaches were built, with toughened panes of glass in the roof.

Before the introduction of steamships it used to take between thirty and thirty-six days to carry mail between the USA and Britain by sailing ship. However by 1840 the new steamships were much faster and made the same journey in around twelve days.

Jesse James and his gang were well-known mail train robbers.

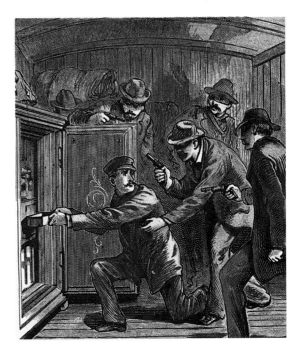

THE PENNY POST

Until 1840 mail was very expensive to send. The cost was based on how many sheets of paper made up the letter and on the distance it had to travel. Postage was paid by the people who received the letters. If the person could not afford to pay, he or she would often refuse to accept the letter. This led to growing demands for a cheaper and simpler postal service.

In 1837 Rowland Hill, an Englishman, suggested that the cost of postage should be paid by the person sending a letter or parcel. He thought that the price should be based on weight but not on distance.

Sir Rowland Hill.

There were petitions for people to sign in support of the Penny Post.

Hill suggested that a one-penny stamp could be stuck on letters and parcels to show that the postage cost had been paid. The British Government liked Hill's ideas and in 1840 set up the Penny Post.

The new system was simpler and cheaper to operate. The first stamp – the Penny Black – had a picture of Queen Victoria's head on it.

Later the Penny Red stamp was used because the black ink of the postmark stood out well against the red stamp.

When a letter was posted, the post office cancelled the stamp with a postmark. The postmark showed the date, time and place the letter was posted. It also prevented people from using the stamp again.

When the first British stamps were issued, there was no need to print the country's name on them because no other country had stamps. Today, Britain is the only country in the world that has no name on its stamps.

Today's stamps often have colourful designs.

STAMPS AROUND THE WORLD

The first stamps were printed in large sheets of 240, and the post office workers had to cut them apart. In 1854 perforations – tiny holes – were made between the stamps, making it easier to tear off each one. On the back the stamps were coated with a kind of gum called 'cement', which was actually not very sticky.

Stamps are still printed in sheets. They are carefully checked for mistakes.

Other countries soon took up the idea of stamps. The USA issued stamps in 1847, Bermuda in 1848, and France and Belgium in 1849.

Some people have tried to forge stamps. So governments go to a lot of trouble to make stamp designs difficult to copy. They also print stamps on paper that has a special pattern, called a watermark.

Right: This intricate stamp from Hungary was printed in 1972.

THE CHANNEL ISLANDS

In 1940, during the Second World War, the Nazis took over the Channel Islands, off the coast of France. The post office on the Islands began to run out of penny stamps. It was impossible to receive any more because of the war. The problem was solved by cutting twopenny stamps in half diagonally to make two penny ones! These stamps were called 'bisects'.

A bisect.

THE PUBLIC POST-BOX

Before the 1850s in Britain, letters could be posted in a bellman's bag. The bellman got his name from the bell he rang as he walked around the streets. If you missed the bellman you had to take your mail to the nearest post office.

A post-box fixed to a bus, Wales, 1937.

General Post Letter Carrier 1793-1855

Before envelopes were invented, letters were folded over, sealed with wax, and posted in the bellman's bag.

Different ways of posting letters have been used elsewhere. On the island of St. Helena in the Atlantic Ocean letters were 'posted' under huge stones known as post office stones, while in Mossel Bay in South Africa an old shoe was hung up and used as a post-box. In Germany, Holland, France and Austria post-boxes were fixed to

'Travelling' letter boxes on trams and buses were popular in Britain as well as in other European countries.

trams and buses.

The first country to come up with the idea of public post-boxes was France, which already had an excellent postal service. The idea spread to the USA, and in 1825 post-boxes were put up in New York.

In 1852 the first British post-box was set up in St. Helier, Jersey on the Channel Islands. It was much easier to slip letters through the slot of a post-box on the street than to

make a trip to the post office. Mail was collected from the post-boxes by post office workers and taken to a sorting office, where it was sorted by hand according to the town and country to which the letters were addressed. Letters would then travel by road, rail or ship to the end of their journey.

Blue painted mail boxes in Boston, USA.

THE PONY EXPRESS

The first American postal system was set up in Boston in 1639. As more European settlers arrived, they built better roads and set up more postal routes. But the USA is a vast country – 4,162 kilometres from New York in the east across to California in the west.

There were soon mail routes from New York as far west as St. Joseph, Missouri. But further west lay a barrier of desert and mountains. Mail between the coasts had to be carried by sea, which took a very long time.

Right: Pony Express Riders in 1861, Billy Richardson, Johnny Frye, Charlie Cliff and Gus Cliff.

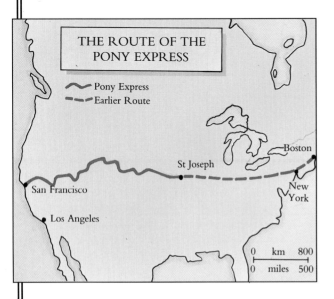

THE ROUTE OF THE PONY EXPRESS

～ Pony Express
- - - Earlier Route

Boston
St Joseph
San Francisco
New York
Los Angeles

0 km 800
0 miles 500

In 1860 the Pony Express Company was formed to carry letters overland between St. Joseph and Sacramento, California, along a trail 3,200 kilometres long.

About a hundred small men and boys, who did not weigh much, rode strong, fast horses, carrying the mail in specially made leather boxes. The Pony Express charged five dollars for a letter weighing half an ounce.

It took ten days and several riders to cover the route. 'Home stations' were placed 120 to 160 kilometres apart. Each rider travelled full speed from one home station to the next, changing horses at small stations in between. When he reached the home station, he quickly handed the mail over to the next rider.

The expert riders avoided fighting when they could, relying on the speed of their ponies to carry them away from trouble.

Being a Pony Express rider was a dangerous job. The riders were often caught in fighting between European settlers and Native Americans. They also had to ride through bad weather conditions.

When the railway was built across the USA, trains were able to carry the mail from coast to coast. The Pony Express was no longer needed and stopped trading after only two years in business.

UNUSUAL DELIVERY

Over the years letters have been carried by every form of transport – canoes, camels, dog sleds, donkeys, skis and hot-air balloons. In Landes, France, letter carriers have even walked on tall stilts to carry mail through marshy ground.

Above: Mail is carried down by mule to the people living at the bottom of the Grand Canyon, USA.

Postal workers in remote areas in the French Alps delivered mail on skis. This picture was painted in 1911.

People living in the Havasupai Native American reservation, deep in the Grand Canyon in the USA, still receive their mail by mule. A steep twelve kilometre trail is the only way in and out of Supai.

The very first air mail was carried not by plane but by carrier pigeon. During the Franco-Prussian war in 1870, Paris was surrounded by Prussian soldiers. No mail was allowed into, or out of, the city. But the French found a way to send messages.

Homing pigeons were flown out of the city by balloon. When important letters needed to be sent to Paris, they were slipped under rings on the pigeons' legs, and the birds were set free to fly home. Altogether they carried more than 2.5 million messages in eighteen weeks.

Carrier pigeons were used during the Franco-Prussian war to carry messages.

WATER MAIL

In 1968, a metal ball used to float letters down river into Paris during the war of 1870 was found in mud from a river bed. The ball contained several hundred letters. The Paris Post Office gave the letters back to the man who found them. He was ordered to keep them until 1998 in case any living relatives turned up to claim them.

Mail sent down river in a container in Florida, USA, 1935.

INTERNATIONAL MAIL

Sending mail to another country used to be very complicated because each country handled mail in a different way. In 1874 people from many countries met to discuss the problems. They agreed to work together and follow the same rules on international mail.

They formed what later became the Universal Postal Union. Thanks to this union, mail could be sent very easily across vast distances. One mail route went from Moscow across Russia on the Trans-Siberian railway, then by sea to China and on to Japan.

Ships still carry a lot of mail although delivery takes much longer than by air.

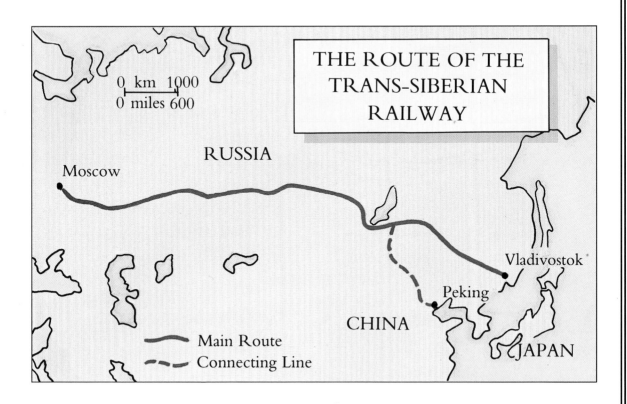

THE ROUTE OF THE TRANS-SIBERIAN RAILWAY

0 km 1000
0 miles 600

RUSSIA

Moscow

Vladivostok

Peking

CHINA

JAPAN

—— Main Route
- - - Connecting Line

The invention of the aeroplane speeded up the delivery of overseas and long-distance mail. In the USA a regular mail service was set up between New York and Washington, DC, in 1918. The following year a service began between Paris and London. Today, a letter can travel from Europe to Australia by plane in two days.

Right: Mail being loaded on a scheduled airline for speedy delivery.

HIGH-SPEED SORTING

In the past post office workers had to sort letters by hand, reading each address. Today, machines sort the mail.

Many countries now use post-codes in their addresses. These pinpoint an address to within a few houses. Post-codes were first used in Britain in 1959. ZIP (Zone Improvement Plan) codes were set up in the USA in 1963. The code identifies the state, city, and delivery area where the letter is going.

Post codes on letters and parcels can be read by the machines in sorting offices. This has increased the speed of sorting.

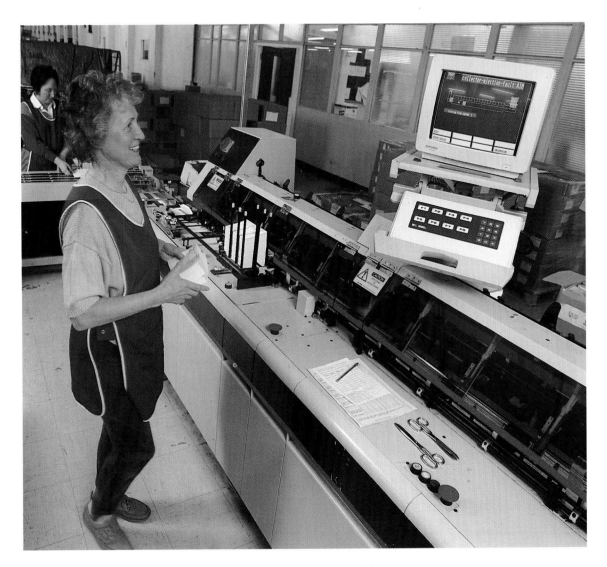

Computers are used to aid the speedy delivery of mail.

Post-codes make it easier and faster for machines to sort mail. An electronic eye 'reads' the post-code. Then thin lines, which set out the address in a special code are sprayed on to the envelope.

Another machine reads these lines and sorts the letters into boxes, according to their address. US-designed high-speed machines can sort more than 30,000 letters in less than an hour.

STAMP COLLECTING

Soon after postage stamps were invented, people began to collect them. Stamp collecting is called philately, and people who collect stamps are called philatelists.

Most stamps are perfect. But, very rarely, mistakes are made. In 1967 a four-cent Cook Islands water lily stamp had 'walter lily' printed on it! This makes stamps more interesting to collectors.

Some collectors only buy stamps that have mistakes on them, like this 'Walter Lily' stamp.

Other stamps are valued by collectors because they are rare. By 1994 a Penny Black in good condition was worth about £85.

WALTER LILY

4^c

COOK ISLANDS

THE RAREST STAMP IN THE WORLD

In 1873 a twelve-year-old boy, Vernon Vaughan, found a purplish red stamp. It was a British Guiana one-cent stamp dated 1856. It was in poor condition, and he later sold it for six shillings.

That stamp turned out to be the rarest stamp in the world. It is the only one of its kind. In 1917 someone bought it for £17,000. Vernon, who was still alive then, must have been amazed! In 1980 the stamp was sold in New York for £400,000. If it were to go on sale today it could fetch between £1 million and £3 million.

If you know someone who receives letters from abroad, they might agree to keep the stamps for you. As your collection grows, you can buy an album to keep your stamps in. Stamps can be damaged by glue, so they should be stuck in with special stamp hinges.

If you are given stamps that are still stuck on an envelope, wet a thick pad of newspaper and put your stamps on top, face upwards, overnight. In the morning the moisture will have loosened them from the paper and you can stick them in your album.

Anyone can be a stamp collector.

TIMELINE

500 BC Early postal routes created throughout the Persian Empire.	**98 AD** The imperial postal system links countries of the Roman Empire.	**476** The Roman postal system comes to an end with the fall of Rome.		**1000-1100** European universities, monasteries and merchants set up postal routes.
1400-1500 Postal routes are common throughout Europe.	**1635** A public postal service is begun between London and Scotland.	**1639** The first American postal system is set up in Boston.	**1825** The First US public post-box is put up in New York.	**1837** Rowland Hill suggests changes to the British postal service.
1838 Steam trains are used to carry British mail.	**1840** The first postage stamp in the world is issued in Britain – the Penny Black.	**1847** The first US postage stamps are issued.		**1852** The first British post-box is set up in St. Helier, Jersey.
1854 Perforations are are added to improve sheets of stamps.		**1860** The Pony Express riders begin to carry mail from the East to the West Coast of the USA.	**1861** The development of the telegraph and rail systems across the USA bring an end to the Pony Express.	**1864** A specially-equipped railway mail coach runs between Chicago and Iowa in the USA.
1874 The Universal Postal Union is formed.	**1918** A regular air mail service is set up in the USA between New York and Washington, DC.	**1919** The first air mail service begins in Europe between London and Paris.	**1963** Zip codes are introduced in the USA.	**1983** Computerised sorting machines are introduced in Britain.

BOOKS TO READ

Club 99 - Write Away by Viv Edwards
(A & C Black, 1991)

A History of Britain's Post by Nance Fyson
(Young Library, 1992)

In the Post by Ruth Thomson
(A & C Black, 1990)

The Post Office Project Book by Jean Barrow
(Watts Books, 1993)

Stamp Collecting by George Beal
(Kingfisher Books, 1986)

The Letterbox by Jean Young Farrugia
(Centaur Press, 1969)
This book is recommended by the Letterbox Study Group and can be found in many public libraries.

PLACES TO VISIT

National Postal Museum
King Edward Building
King Edward Street
London EC1A 1LP
England

Melbourne GPO
Corner Bourke & Elizabeth Streets
Melbourne VIC 3000
Australia

National Postal Museum
Smithsonian Institution
Washington, DC 20560-0001
USA

Toronto's First Post Office and Museum
260 Adelaide Street East
Toronto
ON M5E 1N1
Canada

ADDRESS FOR FURTHER INFORMATION

Mrs Sally Jones (Secretary)
The Letterbox Study Group
43 Miall Road
Hall Green
Birmingham B28 9BS
England

INDEX

Numbers in **bold** indicate subjects shown in pictures as well as in the text.

GLOSSARY

Criminal A person who has done something that is against the law.

Design A pattern or drawing.

Diagonally From corner to corner.

Forge To make an illegal copy of something.

Highwayman A person on horseback who robbed travellers.

International Between countries.

Mail coach A carriage drawn by horses along a road and used to carry post; or part of a train where post is sorted.

Native Americans The people who lived in America before the European settlers arrived.

Papyrus An early kind of paper made in ancient Egypt from papyrus reeds.

Posts Signs, often made out of wood or metal, used to mark the way along a route.

Royal mail A postal system run by the king or queen of a country.

Settle Make a home in a new country or area.